Copyright © 2014 Dr Kartinah Ayupp

All rights reserved.

ISBN:1505645166

ISBN-13:978-1505645163

STRATEGIES FOR IMPROVING KNOWLEDGE SHARING AMONG IT WORKERS

Kartinah Ayupp

Jong Thai Loi

CHAPTER 1

INTRODUCTION

1.1. Introduction

According to Porter and Ketels (2003), information and knowledge sharing provide value-added benefits because it create a synergic effect for developing countries to compete in the global economy. In the early 90s, only a few could see the potential of Information Technology to boost the economic strength of a nation, especially developing countries. One of them is the Malaysian former Prime Minister, Tun Dr. Mahathir Muhammad, who, during the tabling of the Sixth Malaysia Plan in 1991 has announced his wish for Malaysia to be a Knowledge-based Economy. In order to achieve a developed nation status (Vision 2020), a series of plan and activities has been introduced. One of them is the Multimedia Super-Corridor (MSC) which has attracted numerous local and international investors to invest in Information and Communication Technology (ICT) endeavors in Malaysia. This drive has created a huge demand for knowledgeable workers in this area and the starting of the Information Technology (IT) era in Malaysia.

IT workforce which include professionals such as Chief Information Officers, IT Managers, IS Executives, System Analyst, Programmers, Graphic Designer, Database Administrator, IS Support Staffs, IT lectures etc., are recognized as 'knowledge workers' by Neweil et. al. (2002). They are characterized by higher levels of education, have specialist skills and the ability to apply their skills to identify and solve operational problems. Smith and Rupp (2004) also point out that these knowledge workers are employed not just to create or manage a tangible product and/or service, but rather to gather, develop, process and apply information that generates profit to the organization. However, the IT field is so fast moving that if the knowledge possessed by IT workforce is not updated regularly, it will soon become obsolete. Thus, to enhance one's ability and knowledge, IT workers have to share their knowledge with each other, and through this exchange of ideas it can create new knowledge which benefits all. As stated by Kartinah Ayupp and Anandan Perumal (2008), only when the employees are willing to work together as a team can they create a greater synergy for knowledge gain to increase organizational performance and also employee competencies. Unfortunately, this might be easier in the western countries that apply openness in knowledge sharing (Western Centric), but not so in many Asian-based organizations by their lack of adoption of a high level of "share-centric" culture. As quoted by Chowdhury (2006):

"Employees will always be conscious of the appropriateness of their contributions; superiors on the other hand would be cautious to ensure that their comments do not reveal their lack of familiarity of the subject. The result is a very sterilized; and possibility superficial exchange that betrays the whole idea of knowledge-sharing."

This work culture scenario can create problem in the Malaysian IT industry which relies heavily on knowledge and information sharing among organizational members to do their work effectively and efficiently. With this in mind, this study aims to find answers for the following research questions:

RQ1. Is there a significant relationship between the knowledge sharing tendency and organizational factors, such as working environment, supervisors influence and social interaction?

RQ2. Is there a significant relationship between knowledge sharing tendency and personal factors, such as individual's attitude and intention?

RQ3. Does the usage of ICT utilities have direct effects in promoting knowledge sharing tendency among IT workforce?

RQ4. Do demographic characteristics have a direct impact on the knowledge sharing tendency?

Conceptual Framework

A conceptual framework model with essential key constructs and the demographic parameters from Lau's research was slightly modified and further adopted in this research (Lau, E. K-W., 2007).

Figure 1: Theoretical Framework

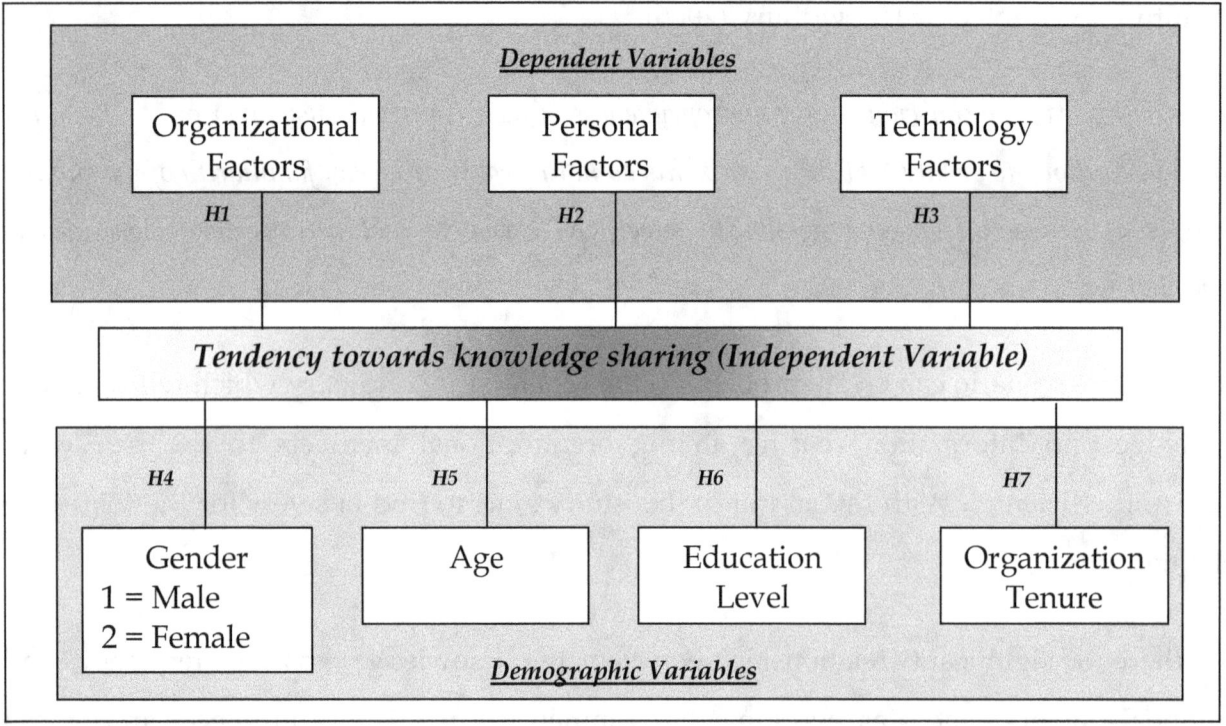

Significance of research

The study aims to identify the factors affecting knowledge sharing, their tendency and impediments among the Malaysian IT workers. Based on the results, the researchers have come up with recommendations that hopefully would improve the ways IT workers share knowledge for better knowledge creation and transfer. They can also be used as general guidelines for management to overcome barriers of knowledge sharing and at the same time raise the awareness and benefits of knowledge sharing to create synergy effects. This can enhance employee retention rates by recognizing the value of employee's knowledge and rewarding them for it. The study results can directly contribute to a larger body of literature on factors that might encourage or hinder knowledge sharing activities. This will increase management understanding of the significance of fostering innovation by encouraging the free flow of ideas and knowledge. At the same time, it can be part of the management's methods and strategies to streamline operations and reduce costs by eliminating redundant or unnecessary processes.

1.4. Scope of research

The study was carried out to analyze the relationship between dependents variables (organizational factors, personal factors and technological factors) as well as demographic variables (age, gender, level of education and job tenure) against the independent variables which are the tendency towards knowledge sharing based on theoretical framework listed in Figure 1 above. The respondents of this research consisted of programmers, database administrators, an IT project manager, Chief information Officer (CIO), Information System executives, IT Trainers, IT lecturers, IT support staffs and other knowledge workers involved in the IT industry. Kuching has been selected as the study area as Kuching is the capital of the East Malaysian state of Sarawak. The population is around 579,900 and consists of multi races such as Malay, Chinese, Indian and the Dayaks including Ibans, Bidayuhs, Melanaus and Orang Ulu, among others. The research examined the factors that influence the knowledge sharing tendency. Data collection was done by distributing the questionnaires to IT respondents around the Kuching area. 200 sets of questionnaires were distributed and 187 have been successfully collected.

CHAPTER 2

LITERATURE REVIEW

2.1. Introduction

According to Nonaka (1994), knowledge can be classified as "tacit" and explicit". Tacit knowledge arises from one's own experiences which includes insights, intuitions, and hunches. Explicit knowledge refers to knowledge that has been expressed into words and numbers. Quinn (1996) described knowledge as one of the most valuable organizational resources possessed by its members. This knowledge includes high-level technical capabilities, practical knowledge, creative abilities and even perceptions of systems. It originates from a person as a result of a combination of his/her own existing knowledge and the in-flow of new information. (Fahey and Prusak, 1998). The term "Knowledge" is furthered explain by Sarmento (2005) as the valuable asset resulting from the combination of data and information, complimented with expert opinion, skills and experience. It is important that this kind of valuable asset is used to aid decision making. Bender and Fish (2000), illustrated the hierarchy of knowledge as Figure 2. Expertise and knowledge both reside in a person and the only differences between knowledge and expertise is that expertise is individualized while knowledge is transferable.

As for knowledge sharing, Lee (2001) defined it as activities of transferring or disseminating knowledge (including implicit and tacit knowledge) from one person, group or organization to another. Cathering (2003) further defined knowledge sharing as a set of behavior that involves the process of exchanging information or assistance to others. How knowledge sharing differs from information sharing is that it contains an element of reciprocity, while information sharing typically involves top management making information available to everyone at every level. Information sharing can be undirectional and unrequested. Porter and Ketels (2003) stated that information and knowledge through collaboration and sharing create a synergic effect as key to value-added which enable developing countries to be able to compete in the growing global knowledge economy. It also a viable approach to reduce duplication of data handling and collection as (Dawes, 1996).

2.2. Factors that encourage or hinder knowledge sharing

According to Kelloway and Barling (2000), social interaction for the sake of knowledge, and unhindered by status or rank, could produce positive knowledge sharing behaviors. They further stated that, building trust between organizational members could encourage them to share knowledge for a better performance. Proper alignment of work process and recognition by the organization could effectively motivate people to share knowledge (McDermott and O'Dell, 2001). This kind of practice shows that management values sharing of knowledge, and is willing to recognize/reward members for the time and effort they spend in this knowledge endeavours. Sometimes legal terms and policy introduced by an organization could also become a reason to permit or prohibit the knowledge sharing process. People are afraid to share the wrong knowledge and so avoid risk. However, this could be easily solved if the organization properly states a policy guidance about who can access what type of information. This also helps in resolving issues related to risk taking, trust development, and at the same time promoting a knowledge sharing culture. (Lane and Bachmann, 1996)

2.2.1. Supervisor/management motivation

One cannot force others to share their knowledge. Thus, management should encourage win-win situations by creating a system that focuses on increase of job-efficiency and cooperation to initiate knowledge workers taking part in the knowledge sharing process (Huysman (2002). Furthermore, managers should be more tolerant towards risk taking behavior and not punish workers who make mistakes in the pursuit of attaining new ways of doing things. Instead of covering up, putting the blame on others and thus negative reinforcement, they should encourage them to learn from the mistake. This is because according to De Long and Fahey (2000):

"...capturing, evaluating, and learning lessons from past mistakes affect best practices in the future."

A supervisor should be taking a facilitator or moderator role to encourage knowledge sharing in teams (Ellinger and Bostrum, 2002). By doing this, a supervisor can develop a high quality collective learning capability, since they are the intermediaries between the operational workers/implementers and top level management. By their status, they can easily influence both learning and change (MacNeil, 2003). However, this middle-management should avoid taking an autocratic approach since this could produce negative effects and alienate workers. The challenge to supervisors is to introduce a suitable medium in which members of the team would want to share their knowledge and learned from others in the team.

2.2.2. Communication flow

Without trust, it is very unlikely one will want to engage knowledge sharing behaviors with others. When there is a culture of trust in the organization, knowledge workers will be confident that whatever knowledge they impart will not be misused, and the knowledge shared is accurate and credible due to the information source. As quoted from De Long and Fahey (2000):

"...level of trust between a company, its sub-units, and its employees seems to have a direct influence on the communication flow and thus the amount of knowledge sharing within and between business functions or subsidiaries"

Riege (2007) suggested that in order to promote knowledge sharing through communication, an organization must create an open communication flow regardless of the hierarchical levels and practices in the organization. Besides that, methods, systems and tools that could benefits or facilitate direct and indirect communication flows should be introduced.

Successful knowledge sharing process depends strictly on one's communication skills, both written and spoken (Hendriks, 1999). In a multiracial nation such as Malaysia, differences in culture or ethnic background are very significant, and diversity of cultures and difference in spoken languages could restrict the knowledge sharing process. Therefore this is one barrier of successful knowledge sharing which management might not foresee and adequately address.

2.2.3. Attitude towards knowledge sharing

Modesty, pride and "saving-face" issues will always reside and take an important place in Asian cultures. (MrDermott and O'Dell, 2001). Asking questions might be seen as a threatening or rude behavior to others. This is because, if the other person could not answer the questions, they might feel they are being humiliated or "losing their face". Furthermore, answering or voicing out opinions in an open discussion might also be perceived as a threatening behavior and can pose a threat to other people's face (pride). Members from high-power distant cultures also tend to avoid being too active in knowledge sharing because they do not want to be perceived as being boastful. The act of knowledge sharing can be further impede by the fact that being too "vocal" is sometimes perceived as trying to jeopardize colleagues' job security.

On the positive side, sharing of knowledge can also lead to a sense or the need for reciprocity. According to Khe and Hara (2006), due to a sense of reciprocity, knowledge workers felt obligated and this drive them to helps others by sharing their knowledge because of past experience where they received help from others. This can create a feeling of responsibility that they should fulfill by sharing their knowledge in return.

2.2.4. Technological factor

Bender and Fish (2000) argued that explicit knowledge which resides in the form of data and information can be distributed with the help of ICT tools and technology such as e-mail, groupware, web forums, Internet, intranet, and videoconferencing with ease of access for all the IT workforce. However, information technology should be seen as a necessary tool to promote knowledge transfer rather than treating it as the core knowledge itself. Cheung and Hew's (2004) further observed that participants sometimes find it hard to express certain ideas clearly in words; and this put them off from contributing what they know. This acts as a hindrance for the knowledge workers to share their knowledge through ICT tools as they felt they have problem of communicating clearly in words and might create misunderstandings to others.

CHAPTER 3

RESEARCH METHODOLOGY

3.1. Research Design

Descriptive and causal research was applied in this study. The research made use of cross-sectional studies to collect raw data and create data structures that describe the existing characteristics of the study objectives. The data was collected and tested to obtain evidence on the variables' cause-and-effect relationships as stated in Figure 1. The propositions based on the conceptual framework are:

- P1: Organizational Factors such as working environment, supervisors influence and social interaction will have positive effect on knowledge sharing.

- P2: Personal factors such as attitude, intention and degree of enjoyment will have impacts towards knowledge sharing

- P3: Technology factors such as ICT facilities will have no significant impact on IT workforce knowledge sharing

- P4: Females are more willing to share knowledge than males.

- P5: Age will have no significant effect on IT workforce's knowledge sharing behavior.

- P6: Education level has no direct impact towards knowledge sharing behavior.

- P7: Number of years spent in an organization will have a significant positive impact on IT workforce's knowledge sharing behavior.

3.2. Population and Sampling

Kuching has been selected as site for the study to be carried on. Kuching is the capital of the East Malaysian state of Sarawak. Elevated to city status on 1st August 1988, Kuching is the largest city on the island of Borneo and the fourth largest city in Malaysia. Kuching is administered and divided into three local government, which are namely DBKU (Kuching North City Hall), MBKS (Kuching South City Council) and MPP (Padawan Municipal Council).

Known as Cat City, Kuching has a population of around 325,132 according to the Malaysian Department of Statistics in 2013. The city have a wide composition of multi-racial ethnic groups such as Malay, Chinese, Indians and the Dayaks (which includes Iban, Bidayuh, Melanau, Kayan and Orang Ulu among others). The main religions are Christianity, Buddhism, Taoism and Islam. Kuching people are generally proficient in Bahasa Malaysia, English and also their own dialects.

3.3. Sampling and Size

200 sets of questionnaires paper were distributed and the aim is to get at least 150 sets of acceptable feedback. This is because it represents the minimum required sample in order to get acceptable level of accuracy. The sample frame consisted of programmers, database administrators, IT project manager, Chief information Officer (CIO), Information System executives, IT Trainers, IT lecturers, IT support staffs and etc. The sampling frame may not have been completely representative of all different kinds of IT workforce, but it was believed that the sample represented the most active users, who were most likely to encounter knowledge sharing issues.

The design of questionnaire included the details of respondents' demography, their knowledge sharing tendency, questions related to organizational factors, personal factors and technological factors. Items in the questionnaire were adapted from previous researches and were used to gauge each of the key variables in the study. The questionnaire was developed in English and organized into three sections:

Table 3.1 Components of Questionnaire

Component	Questions	No. of Questions
Knowledge Sharing Factor		
Tendency	A1, A2, A3	3
Organizational Factors		
Supervisor	B9, B10, B11, B12, B13, B19, B20, B21	8
Interaction	B14, B15, B16, B17. B18	5
Environment	B1, B2, B3, B4	4
Communication	B5, B6, B7, B8	4
Personal Factors		
Intention	B22, B23, B24, B25, B31	5
Enjoyment	B32, B33, B34, B35, B36	5
Attitude	B26, B27, B28, B29, B30	5
Technological Factor		
ICT Facilities	B37, B38, B39, B40, B41, B42	6
Demographic Factors		
Gender, Age, Ethnicity, Education Level, Occupational, Monthly Income, Current Job Tenure	C1, C2, C3, C4, C5, C6, C7	7

The first section which is section A measured the knowledge sharing tendency of respondent through 3 set of questions with the scale ranging from 1 to 5. The 5-points are as following:

1. Strongly Disagree
2. Disagree
3. Neutral
4. Agree
5. Strongly Agree

Section B examined factors related to knowledge sharing. It consists of organizational factors, personal factors and technological factors. Using the same 5-point scale, Questions B1 to B21 measures Supervisor, Interaction, Working Environment and Interaction which all fall under the organizational factors. As for Personal factors, question B22 to B36 measures the Intention, Enjoyment and Attitude factors. Questions B37 to B42 covers aspects of the technological factors. The final section of the questionnaire which is section C examined respondents' demographic information such as age, gender, ethnicity, level of education, Occupational, monthly income and current job tenure fall under questions C1, C2, C3, C4, C5, C6, and C7.

Additionally, several sources of secondary data were gathered through library and Internet, including books and journals articles. These secondary data were useful for problem recognition and analyzing purposes.

3.4. Data Collection

Data collection consists of both primary and secondary data. For secondary data, they consist of data from sources such as published research articles, books, magazines, newspapers etc. For primary data, a set of questionnaire was constructed based on the conceptual theoretical framework and propositions created. The questionnaire was used as a source of the primary data because it enables the researcher to collect considerable quantities of detailed data. However, a level of trust has to be put in the honesty of the respondents as they may be inconsistent, dishonest or inattentive.

A total of 187 responses out of 200 of distributed questionnaire were obtained, representing a response rate of about 93.5%. However, after data processing, only 163 set of responses are considered valid and complete. 24 set of questionnaires were discarded because of missing data or multiple answers in the same question which are considered incomplete. This means only 81.5% of the response rates are complete and valid. In terms of gender, 48.5% were male, while the rest (51.5%) were female. In terms of age, 46.6% of the respondents were within the range of 20-29 years old, 47.9% were in the range of 30-39. Majority of the respondents were Chinese (65%), and most of the respondents have worked for the same company for 5 to 9 years.

3.5. Data Analysis Method

The data collected was analyzed through descriptive statistics by first doing factor analysis to reduce the number of variables to a meaningful and manageable set of factors as well as detecting structure in the relationships between variables. This is to classify variables before reliability test is carried out through Cronbach's alpha testing. Cronbach's alpha should be at least 0.70 or higher to retain an item in an "adequate" scale. Correlation analysis through Pearson method was then undertook to assess the strength of the relationship between the variables. Lastly, regression analysis was done to examine the relationship between the dependent variable and independent variables for testing the research propositions.

CHAPTER 4

FINDINGS

4.1. Summary of Demographic Profile

Table 4.1: Demographic Profile of Respondents

Demographic Variable	Category	Respondent (N = 163)	
		Frequency	(%)
Gender	Female	84	51.5
	Male	79	48.5
Age	20 – 29	76	46.6
	30 – 39	78	47.9
	40 – 49	6	3.7
	Above 50	3	1.8
Ethnicity	Malay	26	16.0
	Chinese	106	65.0
	Indian	5	3.0
	Others	26	16.0
Education Level	High School	32	19.6
	Diploma	18	11.0
	Bachelor's Degree	82	50.3
	Post-Graduate Degree	17	10.4
	Professional Qualification	5	3.2
	Others	9	5.5
Occupational	Professional	16	9.8
	Executive	80	49.1
	Manager	12	7.4
	Clerk/Officer	23	14.1
	Self employed	7	4.3
	Others	25	15.3
Monthly Income	Below RM2000	44	27.0
	RM2001 – RM3000	33	20.2
	RM3001 – RM4000	57	35.0
	RM4001 – RM5000	18	11.0
	RM5001 – RM6000	3	1.8
	Above RM6000	8	4.9
Current Job Tenure	Less than 2 years	29	17.8

	2 – 4 years	36	22.1
	5 – 9 years	65	39.9
	10 – 20 years	31	19.0
	More than 20 years	2	1.2

This section describes the characteristics of the respondents gathered which are summarized in the table above. 163 respondents' demographic details in the aspect of Gender, Age, Ethnicity, Education Level, Occupational, Monthly Income and Current Job Tenure are tabulated for further analysis. It is found that female and male respondents are equally distributed, that is, 51.5% and 48.5% respectively. Majority of them are between the age group of 30 to 39 which comprises of 47.9% of the total respondents. This shows that IT workforce comprised of a relatively young workforce which may be due to the Malaysian government's drive towards the IT sector during early 90s. As for ethnicity, majority of the respondents are Chinese (65%). This followed by Malay and races that comprises of the Sarawak's native such as Iban, Bidayuh, and Malanau. With respect to their education backgrounds, 82 respondents (50.3%) have tertiary education with Bachelor Degree attainment. As for High School leavers, there are total of 32 respondents which comprises of 19.6% of the respondents. This is not surprising since IT workers are considered knowledge workers that possess relatively higher education levels compared to other sectors' manpower. In terms of the respondents' position within the organization, executives constitute 49.1%. This tallies with their education level since to be eligible for executive level's posts, the workers would need at least a bachelor degrees' qualification. This is closely followed by Clerk/Officers post (14.1%), professionals (16%) and managers (12%) of the respondents. In terms of their monthly income, 27% of respondents earned below RM2000 each month, 20.2% are getting around RM2001 to RM3000 and 35% generate a monthly income between RM3001 to RM4000. Only 1.8% has the salary range of RM5001 to RM6000 and 4.9% of respondents have salary that exceeds RM6000 per month. In terms of tenureship, a large number of the respondents have been with the organization between 5 to 9 years (39.9%), followed by those that have worked for 2 to 4 years (22.1%).

4.2. Factor Analysis Result for Knowledge Sharing

Three items of knowledge sharing tendency were submitted to a varimax rotated principal component analysis. The Kaiser-Meyer-Olkin (KMO) measure of sampling adequacy produce a value of 0.702 with Bartlett's Test of Sphericity value of 158.050 and p = .000 further signified the statistical support. The three items submitted were related to knowledge sharing tendencies. As expected, the analysis only produced one significant factor that yielded eigenvalue of 2.158, which represent 71.94% of the variance.. All items were loaded on a single factor of which is termed as "Tendency towards knowledge sharing" (further represent by the term "TENDENCY"). No item was excluded from further analysis and the alpha value for the job satisfaction items was 0.804, which showed good internal consistencies and reliability. The items and the factor loadings were presented in Table 4.2.

Table 4.2: Factor Analysis result for Tendency towards Knowledge Sharing

		Component 1
1	I share my knowledge if people ask me for it	.858
2	I share my knowledge to anyone regardless the trust	.871
3	I share knowledge even if my knowledge is not impressive	.815
Eigenvalue		2.158
Percentage variance explained		71.942
Cronbach's Alpha		0.804
Kaiser-Meyer-Olkin (KMO) measure of sampling adequacy		0.702
Bartlett's Test of Sphericity		158.050
Bartlett's Test of Sphericity Significant		.000

Extraction Method: Principal Component Analysis

a. 1 components extracted

4.3. Factor Analysis Result for Organizational Factors

Twenty-one items which are related to Organizational Factors were submitted to a varimax rotated principal component analysis. The Kaiser-Meyer-Olkin (KMO) measure of sampling adequacy produce a value of 0.828 with Bartlett's Test of Sphericity value of 1955.128 and p = .000 further signified the statistical support. As a result, the analysis produced four significant factors with eigenvalues more than 1.0, representing 68.83% of the variance. The rest was discarded where the eiganvalues are below 1.0. The higher the absolute value of the loading, the more the factor contributes to the variable. Eight items were highly loaded into a single factor which was identified as "Superior or Immediate supervisor relationship" (further represented by the term "SUPERVISOR") which have the eigenvalues of 7.252 with 34.532% of variance explained. This is followed closely by five items which were loaded into a second component with eigenvalues of 3.062, accounting for 14.579% of the variance. The second loaded factor was entitled "Social Interaction" (further represented by the term "INTERACTION"). The other two components were "Working Environment" (represented by the term "ENVIRONMENT") and "Communication Flow" (represented by the term "COMMUNICATION") which has eigenvalues of 2.463 and 1.889 respectively. Both accounted for 11.727% and 8.994% respectively of variance explained. No item was excluded from further analysis and the alpha value for the job satisfaction items was 0.900, which showed excellent internal consistencies and reliability. The items and the factor loadings were presented in Table 4.3.

Table 4.3: Factor Analysis result for Organizational factors

Rotated Component Matrix

		Component			
		1	2	3	4
9	My supervisor encourages me to come up with innovative solutions to work-related problems	**.748**	.004	.097	.219
10	My supervisor organizes regular meetings to share information	**.736**	.302	-.076	.366
11	My supervisor will always keep me informed	**.810**	.121	.069	.067
12	My supervisor encourages open communication	**.834**	.103	.209	-.032
13	My supervisor shows encouragement by action instead words	**.824**	.019	.144	.003
19	My superior is approachable and friendly	**.525**	.223	.449	-.146
20	Open communication is one characteristic of this organization as a whole	**.639**	.137	.482	-.045
21	We are encouraged to say what we think even if it means disagreeing with people we have to report to	**.539**	.270	.357	.137
14	We have "buddy mentoring system" that helps us building trust	.063	**.819**	-.078	.226
15	Office layout is conductive to meeting people (e.g. chat area)	.031	**.777**	.126	-.023
16	Our organization often organizes social meetings to develop spirit goodwill	.218	**.829**	-.022	.134
17	I like to work here because I feel a sense of belonging to this organization	.276	**.699**	.241	.120

18	I feel happy working here because people in this organization treat me as their "brother/sister"	.251	**.529**	.314	.086
1	Members in this organization are free to share ideas because of the "blame-free" culture	.030	.102	**.731**	.142
2	Members know each other very well and this helps us to share knowledge with each other	.192	-.117	**.759**	.116
3	In this organization, we feel proud if our members are successful in their work	.179	.050	**.758**	.225
4	In this organization, those who excel will become role models for other members	.310	.207	**.593**	.221
5	This organization recognizes/rewards those that share knowledge with colleagues	.164	.172	.340	**.634**
6	This organization conducts internal surveys on how knowledge is being shared	.215	.166	.283	**.673**
7	In this organization, people will not envy the success of other	.009	.189	.137	**.701**
8	In this organization, people will not hoard (hide away) knowledge	-.008	.023	.068	**.786**
Eigenvalue		7.252	3.062	2.463	1.889
Percentage variance explained (68.832)		34.532	14.57	11.72	8.994
Cronbach's Alpha (.900)		.897	.846	.803	.817
KMO measure of sampling adequacy		0.828			
Bartlett's Test of Sphericity		1955.128			
Bartlett's Test of Sphericity Significant		.000			

Extraction Method : Principal Component Analysis

Rotation Method: Varimax with Kaiser Normalization

a. Rotation converged in 8 interations

4.4. Factor Analysis Result for Personal Factors

Fifteen items which are related to 'Personal Factors' were submitted to a varimax rotated principal component analysis. The Kaiser-Meyer-Olkin (KMO) measure of sampling adequacy produce a value of 0.807 with Bartlett's Test of Sphericity value of 1035.986 and p = .000 further signified statistical support. As a result, the analysis produced three significant factors with eigenvalues of more than 1.0, representing 70.86% of the variance. The rest was discarded where the eiganvalues are below 1.0. The higher the absolute value of the loading, the more the factor contributes to the variable. Five items were highly loaded into a single factor which we can be identified as "Intention and Condition which seek for return in favor" (further represented by the term "INTENTION") which have the eigenvalues of 6.039 with 40.287% of variance explained. This is followed closely by five items which were loaded into a second component with eigenvalues of 3.076, accounting for 20.508% of variance explained. The second loaded factor was named as "Degree of Enjoyment in helping others" (further represented by the term "ENJOYMENT"). Final component were "Atitude towards knowledge sharing" (represented by the term "ATITUDE") which has eigenvalues of 1.515 for 10.101% of variance explained. No item was excluded from further analysis and the alpha value for the job satisfaction items was 0.840, which showed good internal consistencies and reliability. The items and the factor loadings were presented in Table 4.4.

Table 4.4: Factor Analysis result for Personal factors

Rotated Component Matrix

		Component		
		1	2	3
22	I like to work with others to develop my skill and knowledge	**.681**	.263	.224
23	I learn a lot from others in this organization	**.783**	.196	.129
24	Working in a team helps me to gain more knowledge rather than working independently	**.855**	.166	.272
25	The pooling of knowledge among staff has resulted in new ideas and solutions for the organization	**.853**	.105	.107
31	Sharing knowledge will not lose my competitive advantages in the organization	**.635**	.264	.264
32	We tend to guide junior members instead of letting them learn from their own experience	.159	**.547**	.074
33	In this organization, people enjoy helping other members	.189	**.792**	.158
34	We help each other to learn new skills regardless of seniority	.190	**.861**	.175
35	We keep team members up-to-date with current information	.073	**.828**	.065
36	In this organization, people tend to share tips to excel at work	.175	**.719**	-.200
26	I prefer voluntarily offer my knowledge to all	.233	-.040	**.811**
27	I do not mind to share my knowledge even I will lose ownership of it	.290	.152	**.672**
28	I do not mind to share knowledge which is not common to others	.132	.099	**.620**

29	I do not mind share knowledge even with people I do not particularly like	.031	-.037	**.845**
30	I do not mind to share knowledge with those who are more senior/experienced than me	.140	-.119	**.813**
Eigenvalue		6.039	3.076	1.515
Percentage variance explained (70.866)		40.287	20.508	10.101
Cronbach's Alpha (.840)		.844	.816	8.11
Kaiser-Meyer-Olkin (KMO) measure of sampling adequacy		.807		
Bartlett's Test of Sphericity		1035.986		
Bartlett's Test of Sphericity Significant		.000		

Extraction Method : Principal Component Analysis

Rotation Method: Varimax with Kaiser Normalization

a. Rotation converged in 8 interations

4.5. Factor Analysis Result for Technological Factor

Six items of knowledge sharing tendency were submitted to a varimax rotated principal component analysis. The Kaiser-Meyer-Olkin (KMO) measure of sampling adequacy produce a value of 0.789 with Bartlett's Test of Sphericity value of 384.071 and p = .000 further signified the statistical support. The three items submitted were related with knowledge sharing tendencies. As expected, the analysis only produced one significant factor that yielded eigenvalue of 3.277, which represent 54.62% of the variance. The higher the absolute value of the loading, the more the factor contributes to the variable. All items were loaded on a single factor of which we can confirm as "ICT Facilities" (further represent by the term "ICT"). No item was excluded from further analysis and the alpha value for the job satisfaction items was 0.833, which showed good internal consistencies and reliability. The items and the factor loadings were presented in Table 4.5.

Table 4.5: Factor Analysis result Technological factor

Component Matrix

		Component
		1
37	I prefer to communicate and share ideas with colleagues via ICT facilities	.635
38	I prefer to locate information from internet rather than directly asking for help from colleagues	.719
39	Email or mailing list are good platform for us to freely disseminate information	.679
40	My organization has a knowledge repository that we use to identify experts	.803
41	My organization provides a database to assist us to search job-related documents	.753
42	My organization provides an online discussion platform that we often use to exchange work-related ideas.	.828
Eigenvalue		3.277
Percentage variance explained		54.625
Cronbach's Alpha		0.833
Kaiser-Meyer-Olkin (KMO) measure of sampling adequacy		0.789
Bartlett's Test of Sphericity		384.071
Bartlett's Test of Sphericity Significant		.000

Extraction Method: Principal Component Analysis

a. 1 components extracted.

4.6. Correlation Analysis

Correlation analysis is a technique that is being used to assess the strength of the relationship between two variables. This method was employed in this study to measure the relationship between knowledge sharing tendency against factors such as Organizational Factors, Personal Factors and Technological factors. The results of the correlation analysis were summarized and presented in table 4.6.

Table 4.6: Correlation Analysis – Pearson Correlation Matrix

N = 163	1.	2.	3.	4.	5.	6.	7.	8.	9.
Supervisor									
Interaction	.440(**) .000								
Environment	.479(**) .000	.279(**) .000							
Communication	.329(**) .000	.342(**) .000	.460(**) .000						
Intention	.348(**) .000	.225(**) .004	.504(**) .000	.047 .551					
Enjoyment	.430(**) .000	.372(**) .000	.575(**) .000	.295(**) .000	.480(**) .000				
Attitude	.095 .226	.001 .994	.107 .174	-.221(**) .005	.524(**) .000	.198(*) .011			
ICT	.253(**) .001	.206(**) .008	.063 .428	.277(**) .000	-.024 .765	.100 .203	-.066 .401		
Tendency	.126 .109	.097 .220	.188(*) .016	.222(**) .004	.138 .079	.245(**) .002	-.160(*) .041	.053 .506	
No. of Item	8	5	4	4	5	5	5	6	3

** *Correlation is significant at the 0.01 level (2-tailed).*

* *Correlation is significant at the 0.05 level (2-tailed).*

Table 4.6 indicated that the correlations outcomes SUPERVISOR against other related components were moderately associated with the r value ranging from 0.253 to 0.479 and relatively significant (p < 0.01). Only two components ATTITUDE and TENDENCY are not associated with SUPERVISOR. (p > 0.05). This is also valid for the component INTERACTION against other related components which moderately associated with the r value ranging from 0.206 to 0.440 and relatively significant (p < 0.01). Only two components ATTITUDE and TENDENCY are not associated with INTERACTION. (p > 0.05). As for component ENVIRONMENT, only 2 components are not correlated with it, which are components ATTITUDE and ICT who shown a p value of more than 0.05 and the r value of 0.107 and 0.063 respectively. Other components shows weak to moderate association with the component ENVIRONMENT with r value ranging from 0.188 to 0.575 and significance of p < 0.05 and p < 0.01. There is a moderate negative correlation between COMMUNICATION, and ATTITUDE is found weak with r value of -0.221 and p < 0.01. Other than that, COMMUNICATION has moderate positive correlation against SUPERVISOR, INTERACTION, ENVIRONMENT, ENJOYMENT, ICT and TENDENCY with r value ranging from 0.222 to 0.460. INTENTION is found to have a weak to moderate correlation with all organizational factor components and personal factors components, with r value ranging from 0.225 to 0.524 and significance of p < 0.01.

As for ENJOYMENT, it is found that only component ICT are not correlated with it. The other components are all associated with the r value ranging from 0.198 to 0.575, and a mixture of significant value (p < 0.05, p < 0.01). ATTITUDE correlated with other Personal Factors component such as INTENTION (r value = 0.198; p < 0.05) and ENJOYMENT (r value = 0.524, p < 0.01). There is also a negative correlation associated with COMMUNICATION with r = -0.221, p < 0.05 and TENDENCY, where the r value is -0.198, p < 0.01. Lastly, TENDENCY was found to be positively correlated to ENVIRONMENT, COMMUNICATION and ENJOYMENT with r value of 0.188, 0.222, and 0.245 respectively. There is also a negative correlation with ATTITUDE whereby the r value is -0.160 and correlation is significant at the 0.05 level.

4.7: Regression Analysis

Table 4.7 Regression Analysis for Factors influencing Knowledge Sharing tendency

	Standardized beta coefficients	Sig.	R Square	Adjusted R Square	R Square Change	F Value
Organizational Factors						
Supervisor	.083	.109	.016	.010	.016	2.597
Interaction	.097	.220	.009	.003	.009	1.516
Environment	.188(*)	.016	.035	.029	.035	5.907
Communication	.222(**)	.004	.049	.044	.049	8.369
Personal Factors						
Intention	.138	.079	.019	.013	.019	3.125
Enjoyment	.245(**)	.002	.060	.054	.060	10.262
Attitude	-.160(*)	.041	.026	.020	.026	4.234
Technological Factors						
ICT	.053	.506	.003	-.003	.003	.445

Note: N = 163; *p < .05, ** < .01

Dependent Variable: TENDENCY

Regression analysis was also run to test the relationship between the variables. It was discovered that for Organizational Factors, SUPERVISOR explains 1.6% of variation in the knowledge sharing tendency, INTERACTION explains 0.9% of variation, ENVIRONMENT and COMMUNICATION both respectively explain 3.5% and 4.9% against knowledge sharing tendency. According to the regression table 4.7, it is found that all ENVIRONMENT and COMMUNICATION components listed are positively related to TENDENCY. The beta value for ENVIRONMENT was 0.188, $P< 0.05$ whereas beta value for the COMMUNICATION component was (0.222, $p<0.01$). As for the adjusted R Square value, it has accounted 2.9 % of the variance in the criterion ENVIRONMENT variable and 4.4% for COMMUNICATION in TENDENCY. As for Personal Factors, INTENTION explains 1.9% of variation, while ENJOYMENT explains 6.0% and lastly ATTITUDE explain 2.6% variance in the knowledge sharing tendency.

According to the regression table, it is found that ENJOYMENT and ATTITUDE components listed are positively related to TENDENCY. The beta value for ENJOYMENT was 0.245, $P< 0.001$. It was found that ATTITUDE also has a direct effect towards knowledge sharing tendency. (Beta= -0.160, $p < 0.05$). As for the adjusted R Square value, it has accounted 5.4% of the variance in the criterion ENVIRONMENT variable and 2.0% for COMMUNICATION in TENDENCY. Lastly, for Technological Factors, ICT explains 0.3% variance in the knowledge sharing tendency. However, there is no significant relationship found between ICT and TENDENCY. The adjusted $R2$ value has accounted -0.03 % of the variance in the criterion variable in knowledge sharing tendency.

4.8. T-Test Analysis

A t-test was used to compare the differences in knowledge sharing tendency between gender factors. On average, females IT workers had more tendencies to share knowledge (M = 3.702, SD = 0.588) than their male counterparts (M = 3.224, SD =0.771). This difference was statistically significant, $p < 0.05$, indicating that higher average tendencies are with the female gender. Hence the proposition P4 which states that females are more inclined towards knowledge sharing than males are accepted. The results are summarized in Table 4.8 and Table 4.9

Table 4.8: Group Statistics for T-Test analysis

Gender	N	Mean	Std. Deviation	Std. Error Mean
Female	84	3.702	.588	.064
Male	79	3.224	.771	.087

Table 4.9: Independent Sample Test for T-Test analysis

	Levene's Test for Equality of variances		T-test for Equality of Means		
	F	Sig.	t	df	Sig. 2-tailed
Equal variances assumed	7.067	.009	4.474	161	.000
Equal variances not assumed			4.438	145.653	.000

4.9. Univariate Analysis of Variance

Table 4.10: Tests of Between-Subjects Effects

Dependent Variable: TENDENCY

Source	Type III Sum of Squares	Df	Mean Square	F	Sig.
Corrected Model	18.307	41	.447	.818	.767
Intercept	386.596	1	386.596	707.928	.000
Education Level	4.096	5	.819	1.500	.195
Job Tenure	.337	3	.112	.206	.892
Age	2.888	3	.963	1.763	.158
Education Level * Job Tenure	4.389	12	.366	.670	.777
Education Level * Age	1.085	5	.217	.398	.850
Job Tenure * Age	1.617	3	.539	.987	.401
Education Level * Job Tenure * Age	2.482	6	.414	.758	.605
Error	66.077	121	.546		
Total	2047.444	163			
Corrected Total	84.384	162			

R Squared = .217 (Adjusted R Squared = -.048)

Univariate Analysis of Variance (ANOVA) was run to investigate the relationship between knowledge sharing tendency (TENDENCY) with demographic variables such as age, current job tenure and Level of education of the respondents. The summary of analysis in Table 4.10 reveals that there is no significant difference between the tendency to share knowledge and all demographic variables (combination groups) that are beyond 0.05 of significance level. Hence, propositions P5 and P6 were accepted. Lastly, proposition P7 which states that the current job tenure of respondents will have a significant positive impact on IT workforce knowledge sharing was rejected.

4.10. Conclusion and Propositions

Table 4.11 Summary of Proposition Testing

	Proposition Statement	*Result*
P1	Organizational factors such as working environment, supervisors influence and social interaction will have a positive effect on knowledge sharing.	**Partially supported**
P2	Personal factors such as attitude, intention and degree of enjoyment will have impacts towards knowledge sharing.	**Partially supported**
P3	Technology factors such as ICT facilities will have no significant impact on IT workforce knowledge sharing.	**Accepted**
P4	Females are more willing to share knowledge than males..	**Accepted**
P5	Age will have no significant effect on IT workforce knowledge sharing behavior.	**Accepted**
P6	Education level has no direct impact towards knowledge sharing behavior.	**Accepted**
P7	Number of years spent in an organization will have a significant positive impact on IT workforce's knowledge sharing behavior.	**Rejected**

There were positive relationships between working environment factors as well as communication factors with knowledge sharing tendency, but no significant relationships between supervisor relationship and interaction with co-workers with knowledge sharing tendency. Therefore P1 was partially supported. P2 was partially supported because throughout the analysis, only level of enjoyment upon sharing knowledge and personal attitude has significant relationship with knowledge sharing tendency. As for technological factor through the usage of ICT Facilities, it is found that there is no significant relationship with knowledge sharing tendency. Thus, P3 was accepted. Additionally, it is found that female IT workers are more willing to share knowledge than their male colleagues. In view of this, P4 was accepted. However, asides from the ones mentioned above, all other demographic variables have no significant relationship with knowledge sharing tendency and we can conclude that P5 and P6 were accepted and P7 rejected.

CHAPTER 5

DISCUSSIONS AND CONCLUSION

5.1. Organizational Factors

Although the results shown that there are no direct connection between knowledge sharing tendency and relationship between supervisors and managers, they can still play a role by encouraging and motivating people in the internal and external value chain to share their knowledge more openly. This is done by overcoming process barriers and at the same time, creating an appropriate communication channels for knowledge sharing to take place. This is because organizations that effectively manage and transfer their knowledge are more innovative and perform better than those they do not (Riege, 2007). This mean that supervisors and manager should avoid managing the team using autocratic command and control style which could produce negative effects. The challenge is to find the right medium in which members of the team would want to impart and receive knowledge in an open and trustful manner.

Mutual understanding, influences to others, communication, reciprocity with each other, the individual's social skill; connection and network are important elements in making a successful social interaction between members in an organization. In order to increase morale and face-to-face contact in an informal atmosphere, organization can consider providing a complimentary common 'work-free" zone for social interaction to take place, or to encourage outside activities. Activities that promote interaction such as family days, reunion functions, sports activities and other social gathering should be organized to build up trust and friendship between members.

The working environment acts as an important element in encouraging knowledge sharing tendency among IT workforce as is shown by the research study's result. Through proper recognition by the organization, this could effectively motivate people to share knowledge. Organizations should formally state out policy guidance about who can access what information and level of confidentiality and nature of the information that should and could be shared. This can also helps in resolving issues related to risk taking, trust development, and at the same time promote a knowledge sharing culture (Lane and Bachmann, 1996). A positive working environment which promotes a "blame-free" culture should be perceived as a positive way for self-improvement and for the organization to advance and grow. Proper recognition and rewards should be given for those who share the right knowledge with their colleagues. Perceptions about management's support for knowledge sharing are necessary for the creation and maintenance of a positive knowledge sharing culture in an organization.

In multiracial nation such as Malaysia, differences in culture or ethnic background should not be the barriers towards knowledge sharing. Since English and Bahasa Malaysia are the common communication languages used among different races in Malaysia, there should not be major communication difficulties encountered.

With a positive working environment and level of trust, through proper communication and understanding, knowledge workers can feel that people they shared their knowledge with will not misuse their knowledge, At the same time their colleagues can assume that the knowledge shared is accurate and credible due to the information source.

5.2. Intention and Attitude towards Knowledge Sharing

As knowledge sharing does not come without costs, personal beliefs that the benefits will outweigh such costs are likely to be an important determinant of knowledge sharing behaviors. Self-interest and personal gain are another consideration when sharing IT knowledge. This is because an individual who chooses to share knowledge not only faces the risk of losing his/her unique value within the organization, but any knowledge shared that was subsequently judged to be unsound/ irrelevant can damage the worker's reputation.

Notwithstanding the above, the study's results shows that knowledge sharing tendencies are not all about monetary rewards or recognition. A lot of the respondents expressed feeling of enjoyment when they shared their knowledge with others. This may be due to the Malaysians nature of kind hospitality and generosity that illicit enjoyment when helping others that includes knowledge sharing as well.

People tend to see knowledge sharing as the means to overcome business problems and/or achieve certain objectives which eventually will benefit all parties concerned. This Asian characteristic appears to help keep the knowledge-sharing spirit strong, because people get their enjoyment from the appreciations shown, such as thankful words, rather than focusing on the lack of monetary rewards/recognition by the organization.

5.3. ICT Facilities

It was interesting to note that, although IT workers are expected to be IT savvy, they seldom used organizational intranet and online collaboration tools for information and knowledge sharing. The result tally with Bender's (2000) and Cheung's (2004) past studies. This fact may be due to the fact that the workers sometimes find it hard to express certain ideas clearly in words; and this put them off from contributing what they know. This ultimately created a barrier for them to share their knowledge through ICT tools because they fear their knowledge will create confusion and misunderstandings to others. For these types of workers, it is found that they prefer face-to-face communication or using communication medium such as telephone when sharing knowledge. This can be very restrictive in the spreading of knowledge because information technology is deemed to be the most efficient and cost-effective tool to promote knowledge transfer throughout the organization.

5.4. Demographics

Demographic variables are shown to have a significant influence on workers' level of knowledge sharing tendencies. This study tallies with Shermerhorn (1977), in the sense that workers with shorter organizational tenure are more likely to share their information. One reason for this is because they want to give a good impression to others, while at the same time to create friendly atmosphere and obtain management's recognition with the aim of building up their reputation in the organization.

As for gender, females are shown to have a higher tendency to share knowledge compared to males. However, management are still advised to provide proper recognition to them because, although females are naturally conditioned to be helpful and kind, they might be hesitant to share knowledge if they believe that sharing knowledge might cause them to lose their competitive edge. Therefore, a positive social interaction culture must be promoted to allow trust to grow for both sexes.

It can be concluded that the Malaysian IT workers have a positive attitude towards knowledge sharing. In comparison to past researches conducted in other western and eastern countries, their knowledge sharing level in term of awareness and tendency is on par with developed countries such as America, United Kingdom, China and Korea.

5.5. Limitation and Recommendation for Future Research

Although the response rate of this study was acceptable (81.5%), the sample size was considered small. Future studies should include larger sample size to increase the accuracy and representativeness of the result. Furthermore, this study only focused on organizational, personal and technological factors to predict the tendency in knowledge sharing. There may be other factors that are particular to each interaction, which can be used to predict a complete scenario on knowledge sharing tendency. Variables such as reward structures, trust, hierarchical structures in the organizations, political behavior and other potential variables should be used in future study.

This study scope could also be broaden to include other industries within the manufacturing and services sectors. It would be interesting to determine if there is similarity or differences in knowledge sharing tendencies in different occupational sectors. Lastly, the study locations should be widen to include other states in Malaysia to yield a more robust & in-depth study of the knowledge sharing phenomenon.

REFERENCES

1. Bender, S. and Fish, A. (2000). The transfer of knowledge and the retention of expertise : the continuing need for global assignments, *Journal of Knowledge Management*, Vol. 4, No.2, pp.125-137.

2. Cheung, W. S., and Hew, K. F. (2004). Evaluating the extent of ill-structured problem solving process among pre-service teachers in an asynchronous online discussion and reflection log learning environment, *Journal of Educational Computing Research*, Vol. 30, No.3, pp.197-227.

3. Chow, C. W., F. J. Deng, and J. L. Ho. (2000). The openness of knowledge sharing within organizations: A comparative study of the United States and The People's Republic of China, *Journal of Management Accounting Research*, Vol. 12, pp. 65-95.

4. Chowdhury, N. (2006). Knowledge management in Malaysia—why sow adaption? Knowledge Board. Retrieved April 23, 2007 from World Wide Web http://www.knowledgeboard.com/item/2643.

5. Connelly, C.E., and Kelloway, E.K. (2003). Predictors of employees' perceptions of knowledge sharing cultures, *Leadership & Organization Development Journal*, pp 294-301.

6. Constant, D., Kiesler, S., and Sproull, L. (1994). What's mine is ours, or is it? A study of attitudes about information sharing, *Information Systems Research*, Vol. 5, pp. 400 – 421.

7. Dawes, S. (1996). Interagency information sharing: expected benefits, manageable risks, *Journal of Policy Analysis and Management*, Vol. 15, No. 3, pp. 377-94.

8. De Long, D.W., and Fahey, L. (2000). Diagnosing cultural barriers to knowledge management, *The Academy of Management Executive*, Vol. 14, No.4, pp.113-27.

9. Ellinger, A.D., and Bostrum, R.P. (2002). An examination of managers' beliefs about their roles as facilitators of learning, *Management Learning*, Vol. 33, No. 2, pp. 147-79.

10. Fahey, L., and Prusak, L. (1998). The eleven deadliest sins of knowledge management, *California Management Review*, Vol. 40, No. 3, pp. 265-76.

11. Hendriks, P. (1999). Why share knowledge? The influence of ICT on the motivation for knowledge sharing, *Knowledge and Process Management*, Vol. 6, No.2, pp.91-100.

12. Huysman, M. (2002). Knowledge Sharing in Practise, Vrije University Amsterdam (http://staff.feweb.vu.nl/mhuysman/).

13. Kartinah Ayupp, and Anandan Perumal (2008), A Learning Organization: Exploring Employees' Perceptions', *Management and Change*, Vol. 12, No. 2, pp. 29 – 46.

14. Kelloway, E.K., and Barling, J. (2000). Knowledge work as organizational behaviour, *International Journal of Management Reviews*, Vol. 2, pp. 287-304.

15. Khe, F.H., and Hara, N. (2006). Identifying factors that encourage and hinder knowledge sharing in a longstanding online community of practice, *Journal of Interactive Online Learning*, Vol. 5, No. 3, pp. 297-316.

16. Lane, C., and Bachmann,R. (1996). The social constitution of trust : supplier relations in Britain and Germany, *Organization Studies*, Vol. 17, No. 3, pp. 365-95.

17. Lau, K.W. (2007). The use of an Online discussion forum for case sharing in business education, *International Journal of Learning Technology*, 3(1), pp.18-31.

18. Lau, K.W., (2006). Factors motivating people toward pirated software, *Qualitative Market Research*, Vol. 9, No.4, pp.404-419.

19. Lee, J.N. (2001). The impact of knowledge sharing, organizational capability and partnership quality on outsourcing success, *Information and Management*, Vol. 38, No. 5, pp.53 23-35.

20. MacNeil, C.M. (2003), The line manager as a facilitator of team learning and change, *HRD in a Complex World*, pp. 218-30.

21. McDermott. R, and O'Dell, C. (2001). Overcoming cultural barriers to sharing knowledge, *Journal of Knowledge Management*, Vol. 5, No. 1, pp 76-85.

22. Nonaka, I. (1994). A dynamic theory of organizational knowledge creation, *Organizational Science*, Vol. 5, No. 1, pp. 14-37.

23. Quinn, J.B., Anderson, P., and Finkelstein, S. (1996). Managing professional intellect: making the most of the best, *Harvard Business Review*, Vol. 74, No. 2, pp. 71-80.

24. Ramus, C. (2001). Organizational support for employees: encouraging creative ideas for environmental sustainability, *California Management Review*, Spring, pp. 85-105.

25. Sarmento, A. (2005), Knowledge management: at a cross-way of perspectives and approaches, *Information Resources Management Journal*, Vol. 18, No. 1, pp. 1-7.

26. Shermerhorn, J.R. (1977). Information sharing as an interoganizational activity, *Academy of Management Journal*, Vol. 21, pp. 148 – 153.

27. Smith A.D., and Rupp W.T (2004). Knowledge workers' perceptions of performance ratings, *The Journal of Workplace Learning*, Vol. 16, No.3, pp. 146-166.

28. So C.F., Johnny, and Bolloju Narasimha (2005). Explaining the intentions to share and reuse knowledge in the context of IT service operations, *Journal of Knowledge Management*, Vol. 9 , No.6, pp 30-41

29. Sven C. Voelpel and Zheng Han, (2005). Managing knowledge sharing in China : The case of Sienmens ShareNet, *Journal of Knowledge Management*, Vol. 9, No.3, pp 51-63

30. Wilms, W.W., Hardcastle, A.J., and Zell, D.M. (1994). Cultural transformation at NUMMI, *Sloan Management Review*, pp. 99-113.

www.ingramcontent.com/pod-product-compliance
Lightning Source LLC
Chambersburg PA
CBHW081800170526
45167CB00008B/3271